Why **EVERY** Adult **MUST** Have A Health Care Directive

Jennifer R. Lewis Kannegieter

© 2013 by Jennifer R. Lewis Kannegieter

All Rights Reserved.

No part of this book may be reproduced, stored in a retrieval system, or transmitted in any form or by any means without the prior written permission of Jennifer R. Lewis Kannegieter.

ISBN-13: 978-1479375707

ISBN-10: 1479375705

This book is intended for informational purposes only.
No part of this book shall be construed as legal advice.
No attorney-client relationship is formed by use of this book.

Table of Contents

Introduction	5
What Is A Health Care Directive?	7
Why Do I Need A Health Care Directive?	11
8 Steps To Advance Care Planning	15
#1 - Learn About Your Treatment Options	17
#2 - Consider Your Values And Wishes	19
#3 - Choose Your Health Care Agent	21
#4 - Provide Your Instructions	27
#5 - Make It Legal!	29
#6 - Talk About It	31
#7 - Make It Accessible	35
#8 - Review And Update It Regularly	37
Appendix A - Additional Resources	39
Appendix B - Free Minnesota Health Care Directive Form with Instructions	41
About The Author	53

Introduction

The Importance of Health Care Directives

Approximately 70% of Americans will face difficult end of life medical decisions. Making these decisions for ourselves is hard, but making these decisions for our loved ones can be heart-wrenching. Chances are you know someone who has been put in the position of needing to make important medical decisions for a dying family member. More often than not these decisions are followed by second-guessing and self-doubt.

Having a Health Care Directive can provide comfort for your family during a difficult time. Most adults know they *"should"* have a Health Care Directive, yet only about 25% actually do have one.

This book will take you through the basics of Advance Care Planning, explain why every adult needs a Health Care Directive, and go through the eight steps to Advance Care Planning. While a Health Care Directive is always included as part of my *Total Estate Planning Packages* and some people do require an attorney's assistance in Advance Care Planning, many people are able to complete a Health Care Directive on their own. I am excited to provide a free Minnesota Health Care Directive form with this book and on our website at www.LewisKLaw.com/mnhcd.

Please share this book with your friends and family. Help me raise awareness about the importance of Health Care Directives. If you have any questions, or if it is time to complete your estate plan, please contact me.

-Jennifer R. Lewis Kannegieter

What Is A Health Care Directive?

Health Care Directive?
Living Will? Medical Power of Attorney?

A Health Care Directive, Living Will, and Medical Power of Attorney are all types of advance medical directives – written documents dealing with medical treatment preferences. These directives are all part of Advance Care Planning. With an advance medical directive you can make legally valid decisions about future medical treatments - treatments that you may receive at a time when you are unable to speak for yourself.

Although there are subtle differences between the documents, the terms are often used interchangeably.

A *Living Will* is a legal document that allows you to provide instructions for the type of care you want to receive if you are unable to make your own decisions. A Living Will should not be confused with a Will or a Living Trust – which are both estate planning tools used to distribute assets.

A *Medical Power of Attorney* or *Durable Power of Attorney for Health Care* is a legal document that allows you to name another person to make medical decisions for you if you are unable to do so yourself.

A *Health Care Directive* combines both the ability to provide instructions and the power to appoint someone to make decisions for you.

In Minnesota, Living Wills were first recognized as a form of advance directive, in 1989. Living Wills applied only to people with a terminal illness who could not communicate their decisions. Durable Powers of Attorney for Health Care were introduced in 1993. In 1998, the Minnesota legislature introduced the Health Care Directive, which has been in use since.

What Is Advance Care Planning?

Advance Care Planning means considering your options, values, and preferences then providing instructions for the health care decisions that may be required in the event of a serious accident or illness, or for your end-of-life care.

Advance Care Planning v. Health Care Directive

Advance Care Planning is the thought process and conversations that happen regarding wishes and preferences for end-of-life medical care. A *Health Care Directive* is the written legal document that allows you to provide instructions for your medical care and/or appoint someone else to make decisions for you.

Advance Care Planning can occur between the would-be patient and loved ones or medical providers. Advance Care Planning can be very specific, or it can be very vague. Advance Care Planning may or may not be in writing. A Health Care Directive puts your wishes and preferences on paper. More importantly, a Health Care Directive makes your Advance Care Planning legally enforceable.

What About A DNR?

There may be some confusion about Health Care Directive and a 'DNR.' A 'DNR' is, quite simply, a Do Not Resuscitate Order. Similarly, a 'DNI' is a Do Not Intubate Order. This is a medical order, signed by a doctor, ordering that certain treatments not be performed. These orders typically come after something has happened, and after a discussion between the doctor and the patient or patient's family about treatment options. A Health Care Directive is prepared in advance, by the patient. And while it is possible to provide instructions supporting a DNR or DNI, a Health Care Directive could also provide instructions to continue all treatments, including resuscitation and intubation, for as long as possible.

Minnesota Legal Requirements

While the name and specific requirements may vary, all states legally recognize some form of advance medical directive. However, each state has its own laws about what is and is not allowed in the directive, and how a directive may be signed, witnessed, and notarized.

Most states recognize legal directives from another state, provided the directive is legally valid in the state in which it was created. However, there may be conflicting laws between states, resulting in invalid provisions or directives. It is always a good idea to check each state's legal requirements if you move to a new state, or even if you plan to spend any considerable time in another state.

To be valid, a Health Care Directive in Minnesota must:

- Be prepared by someone 18 years of age or older with legal capacity;

- Be in writing, signed, and dated;

- Be witnessed by two adults or verified by a notary public;

- Include either the appointment of a Health Care Agent **or** instructions for health care **or** both.

Why Do *I* Need A Health Care Directive?

In 1900 the average life expectancy in the United States was only 47. Most people died quickly from an accident or sudden illness. By 2000, the average life expectancy had increased to 78. Nowadays, most people die slowly from a chronic disease. A few statistics regarding 80-90% of deaths in the United States:

- 20% of deaths follow a cancer pattern – a long illness with decline just before death;

- 30% of deaths follow a dementia pattern – progressively growing more frail over time, possibly up to ten years;

- 30-40% of deaths involve organ system failure – a series of hospitalizations over several years, leading up to death.

Advances in medical technology have provided numerous ways to treat conditions that were previously untreatable. We are now able to prolong life in ways that previous generations could never imagine. In fact, many patients now spend (on average) 8 days in the ICU, comatose or on a ventilator, before death. But for many people, this is **not** the way they wish to spend their last few days.

With medical advances come choices. There can be several different options about how a patient is treated, where they receive care, and for how long those treatments are used. If you are unable to speak for yourself and make those decisions, your doctors will be looking for someone else to make those decisions for you.

A Health Care Directive Protects Your Rights

The federal Patient Self-Determination Act legally protects each person's right to make his or her own medical decisions, including decisions to refuse or withdraw treatment. A Health Care Directive provides the perfect opportunity to exercise this right.

The 1990 US Supreme Court case of *Cruzan* determined that the state of Missouri could require "clear and convincing evidence" of a patient's wishes before removing life support. Family members saying "this is what I think she would want" would *not* be enough. A Health Care Directive providing guidance regarding the patient's wishes could be crucial to establishing the necessary evidence.

A Health Care Directive Protects Your Family

If you are unable to make decisions about your care, your doctors will turn to your family for guidance. The decisions your family might have to make for you are often very difficult and emotional. These decisions may have to be made during a time of crisis. Your family may struggle with the responsibility of these decisions. These decisions may cause disputes between family members. A Health Care Directive can provide your family comfort in knowing what you would want, while preventing disputes between well-intentioned loved ones.

A Health Care Directive Keeps You Out of Court

Every couple of years you hear about a high-profile court case. The patient, and subject of the legal dispute, is seriously ill and unable to speak for themselves. The family members and doctors are fighting about who should make medical decisions and what medical care the patient should (or should not) be receiving. These cases happen every day, we just don't hear about them. A Health Care Directive can provide clear guidance to all of your loved ones and your doctors, eliminating disputes and keeping you out of court.

Why Even Young Adults Need A Health Care Directive

Once your child turns 18 years old (typically during their senior year of high school), he or she is legally considered an adult. If something was to happen to your child and he or she was unable to communicate, you may experience difficulty in getting information about your child's condition or even making decisions about his or her care. You may not even be immediately informed that your child is hospitalized.

So give yourself some peace of mind and have each of your children complete a Health Care Directive as soon as they become a legal adult. Make sure your child always carries emergency contact information. Consider getting a DocuBank membership for your child so you know they are protected.

Remember...

With a Health Care Directive, you can decide what treatment you receive, where you receive it at, and what is considered in your course of treatment.

Without a Health Care Directive, you will receive treatment. However, it may not be the treatment you would choose for yourself.

With a Health Care Directive, you can choose who will speak for you.

Without a Health Care Directive, someone else will have to make decisions about your treatment. However, those decisions may be made by people that you would never want to speak for you.

With a Health Care Directive, your family will have peace of mind knowing things went the way you would have wanted them to.

Without a Health Care Directive, your family may torment themselves over whether or not they made the right decisions.

No one can predict when a serious accident or illness might occur. A Health Care Directive does not need to be permanent. You can always decide to update or revoke your Health Care Directive. You are **NOT** able to decide to get a Health Care Directive when you really **NEED** one.

8 Steps to Advance Care Planning

Advance Care Planning and a Health Care Directive can be completed in just eight simple steps:

1. **Learn About Your Treatment Options** – It is impossible to leave instructions if you do not understand your options.
2. **Consider Your Values and Wishes** – An integral part of Advance Care Planning is knowing and understanding what is most important to you.
3. **Choose Your Health Care Agent** – Choosing the right agent (the person who makes treatment decisions) will provide protection and comfort for you and your loved ones.
4. **Provide Your Instructions** – Health Care Instructions can guide your agents, family, and doctors in making the right choices for you.
5. **Make It Legal!** - A valid Health Care Directive makes sure everyone is on the same page.
6. **Talk About It** – Share your thoughts and wishes about end-of-life care with those closest to you.
7. **Make It Accessible** – A Health Care Directive is no good if it is not there in an emergency. Make sure you keep a copy accessible, and ensure that your agent has a copy of their own.
8. **Review and Update It Regularly** – An out-of-date Health Care Directive can be worse than no Health Care Directive at all.

The following pages of this book will take you through each step, providing you more information and things to consider in your Advance Care Planning. At the end of this book you will find a **free** Minnesota Health Care Directive form (also available online) that you can fill out and complete as a legally valid advance medical directive. There is no reason to delay, nobody is guaranteed a tomorrow. Complete your Health Care Directive; then pass this book on to your loved ones.

#1
Learn About Treatment Options

It is difficult to provide instructions and preferences if you do not understand what your options are. While there is no possible way to address every treatment or procedure that may be considered, there are some common conditions and treatments routinely used in end-of-life situations that you should consider.

Ventilator/Respirator: This is also known as a breathing machine. This is used when you cannot breathe on your own. You cannot talk or eat by mouth while on this machine.

Cardiopulmonary Resuscitation (CPR): This is the process of making your heart and lungs work when they stop. This can include the chest compressions we know as CPR, electric shocks, medications, and a tube in your throat.

Dialysis: The mechanical means of cleaning the blood when your kidneys are not working.

Nutrition and Hydration Support: These are the feeding solutions used to provide enough nutrition to support life indefinitely when you cannot eat or drink by mouth. This can be done with a tube in your stomach, nose, intestine, or veins. In Minnesota this is considered a treatment option and can be withdrawn. Some states do not allow for nutrition and hydration support to be withdrawn.

Vegetative State: A vegetative state is defined as a form of "eyes-open permanent unconsciousness in which the patient has periods of wakefulness and physiologic sleep/wake cycles, but is at no time aware of himself or his environment." A vegetative state occurs when there is severe brain damage. After four weeks in a vegetative state, the patient is classified as being in a *persistent vegetative state*. After one year the patient is classified as being in a *permanent vegetative state*.

Terminal Condition: A status that is incurable or irreversible and in which death will occur within a short time. "A short time" does not have a standard definition, but is generally considered to be less than one year.

#2
Consider Your Values and Wishes

Understanding what is important to you is paramount to Advance Care Planning. Consider asking yourself some of the following questions:

Religious and/or Spiritual Influence

- How would you describe your religious or spiritual life?
- How do your religious and/or spiritual beliefs impact your feelings towards end-of-life care and death?
- What religious or spiritual comforts would you want in your final hours?

What Really Matters?

- What gives your life the most meaning?
- What do you most value about your physical well-being?
- What do you most value about your mental well-being?
- What activities bring you the most joy?

Pain Control

- What are your feelings about pain control?
- Would you rather have your pain well-controlled or be aware of the people around you in your final hours?

Thoughts on Death

- What fears about death do you have?
- What type of care would you like to receive in your last days?
- Who would you want with you in your final hours?
- What would you want most in your final moments?
- If you could plan it, what would your last day or week be like?

What Are The Odds?

- How would the odds of survival impact your decisions? If they were over 85%? Over 50%? 20%? Less than 2%?
- How would the risk of severe side effects impact your decisions?
- Would your feelings change as you age?

A Life Worth Living

- How do you feel about quality-of-life?
- At what point would you feel life is no longer worth living?
- How would you feel if you could no longer do the activities that you enjoy?
- How would you feel if you lost the thing you value most about your physical well-being? Mental well-being?
- What if you could no longer recognize or communicate with your loved ones?

Please Remember Me

- What one thing do you want to make sure your doctors and loved ones know about your wishes?
- How would you like to be remembered after you are gone?
- What would you want your loved ones to do after your death?
- What songs, prayers, or readings would you want at a funeral or memorial service?

#3
Choose Your Agent

What Is A Health Care Agent?

A Health Care Agent is the person, or persons, you select and appoint in your Health Care Directive to speak on your behalf and make decisions about your medical care if you are unable to do so for yourself.

A Health Care Agent must follow any health care instructions included in your Health Care Directive and they must follow any additional instructions or preferences you have provided outside of the directive. A Health Care Agent must act in your best interest. A Health Care Agent has broad powers, including the powers to:

- Make any health care decisions for you when you are unable to do so for yourself. This includes deciding when to give, refuse, or withdraw consent to any care, treatment, service, or procedure.

- Choose where you receive care, including choosing your health care providers and care facilities.

- Choose where you live when you need health care and determine what personal security measures or restraints are needed for your safety.

- Access, review, and disclose your medical records.

- A Health Care Agent's powers can also be limited by the Health Care Directive or you can expand your agent's power in your Health Care Directive to include things such as:

- Make health care decisions for you when you are able to speak for yourself, if you want the agent to do so at that time.

- Arrange for and make decisions about the care of your body after your death, including carrying out your wishes regarding burial, cremation, or donation.

- Determine whether to continue a pregnancy to delivery if you are pregnant at the time of care.

- If you have appointed a spouse or domestic partner, you can grant them the power to continue as your Health Care Agent even if a divorce, legal separation, or termination of the marriage or domestic partnership has started or occurred. (Typically appointments of a spouse or domestic partner are treated as null and void if there has been a court proceeding for divorce or separation since the appointment was made).

A Health Care Directive typically appoints one agent to serve first, and an alternate agent or agents if the first is unable or unwilling to serve when needed. You can appoint one person to act individually or you can appoint more than one person to act as co-agents. If you appoint more than one person, you must decide whether your agents need to act all together and in agreement, or if only one agent is needed to act.

Choosing Your Health Care Agents

In Minnesota there are only two legal requirements for your Health Care Agent: 1.) Your Health Care Agent **must** be 18 years of age or older; and 2.) You cannot appoint a health care provider or an employee of a provider giving direct care to you, *unless* you are related to that person or you have stated a reason why you want that person to serve.

When selecting a Health Care Agent, you should look for someone who:

- Is someone you trust and someone who knows you well.

- Is willing to act on your behalf and carry out your wishes, regardless of if they agree with your wishes.

- Would be close by and available to act in an emergency.

- Can handle making difficult decisions during a difficult time. Would not be easily intimidated or overwhelmed.

- Is someone you feel comfortable sharing your beliefs with and talking about your wishes.

To choose your Health Care Agent(s), first make a list of all the possible candidates. Then rank them based upon how well they fit the above criteria. Consider if you want to name individual agents or co-agents. Before appointing a Health Care Agent it is *always* a good idea to talk to them and make sure they are willing to act and comfortable with being appointed. You can also provide your agents with a copy of the next page explaining their responsibilities as a Health Care Agent.

Serving as a Health Care Agent

If you are appointed as a Health Care Agent it is important to understand what your role is and what you may be required to do. As a Health Care Agent you will be asked to make decisions in the place of the patient. You are to make decisions based upon the directions provided in the Health Care Directive, any additional instructions you have received from the patient, and upon your own understanding of what the patient would want. You are to always act in the best interest of the patient.

As a Health Care Agent, you should be prepared to:

- Receive and review the patient's medical records.

- Talk to the patient's doctors and other care providers, ask questions, and get explanations about treatment options, risks, and benefits.

- Request consults or second opinions.

- Consent to or refuse medical treatments, including treatments that may sustain life.

- Advocate on behalf of the patient. Make difficult decisions. Make decisions based on what the patient would want. Do not let yourself be influenced by others.

- Choose the patient's doctors and where he or she receives care.

If you are appointed a Health Care Agent, make sure you are given a copy of the Health Care Directive. Keep the directive in a safe place where you can easily access it if you are called. If you are called to serve as an agent, bring your copy of the directive along with you to the hospital.

Become familiar with the medical instructions provided in the directive. Do not be afraid to ask the person who has appointed you about his or her preferences, beliefs, and feelings on medical treatment, quality of life, and death. Consider taking notes on these conversations to keep with the directive.

If the Health Care Directive is ever updated, you should be given a copy of the new directive. It is important that you either return the copy of the old directive to be shredded, or shred it yourself.

#4
Provide Your Instructions

The instructions you provide in your Health Care Directive can be as detailed and specific as you want them to be, or you can provide a few general guidelines about your thoughts and feelings towards end-of-life care. If you have appointed a Health Care Agent, you do not even **need** to provide instructions. However, your family and agents will appreciate as much guidance as you can provide about your medical treatment preferences.

In providing instructions, consider the following things:

- **Specific Treatments.** If you have opinions about specific treatment options these should be incorporated into your instructions.

- **Preferences for Organ Donation.** Include any preferences you have regarding organ donation, including what you would and would not want to have donated.

- **Instructions for Arrangements.** You can provide instructions about what you would like done with your body after death, including burial, cremation, or donation. You can also include guidance on any final memorial service.

- **Pregnancy Care.** If there's any possibility you may be pregnant at the time of treatment, consider providing instructions and guidance for your agent on making decisions for both you and your unborn child.

- **Health Care Goals.** What are your overall goals? To live? To maintain a certain quality-of-life? To control pain? To be able to recognize and interact with family and friends? To be able to be physically active?

- **Religious and/or Spiritual Beliefs.** Consider including information on your beliefs if these beliefs have shaped your preferences.

- **Quality-of-life Opinions.** If quality-of-life concerns have shaped your preferences consider incorporating these into your instructions.

- **Thoughts on Death and Dying.** Providing guidance about your thoughts on death can bring your family comfort and peace during a difficult time.

#5
Make It Legal!

While it is possible to do some Advance Care Planning without creating a Health Care Directive, a legally valid directive will provide your family (and yourself) with much needed comfort and protection. Many states have organizations that will provide a free advance medical directive form.

In Minnesota, there is no required Health Care Directive form that must be used. A valid Health Care Directive just needs to:

- Be prepared by someone who is 18 years of age or old, with the legal capacity to do so,

- Be in writing,

- Contain either an appointment of a Health Care Agent **or** instructions for care, **or** both, and

- Be signed and dated and **either** witnessed by two adults **or** notarized by a notary public.

- The witnesses cannot be someone who is named as an agent or alternate agent. Only one witness can be a direct health care provider or employee of a provider.

While a Health Care Directive is typically included as part of an estate plan, you can (and should) have a Health Care Directive even if you do not have any other estate planning documents. Some people may benefit from the assistance of a lawyer in preparing their Health Care Directive, but for most people there is no need for a lawyer.

I have prepared a Minnesota Health Care Directive form that is available on our website and included in the back of this book. Please feel free to use this form in creating your legally valid Minnesota Health Care Directive.

#6
Talk About It

Before completing a Health Care Directive you can have Advance Care Planning conversations with your loved ones. Talk about your thoughts on death and end-of-life care. Talk about who you would want to speak for you and what treatments you would or would not want. Talk about what type of funeral arrangements you would like and whether you would like to be buried or cremated. Talk about every topic you can think of.

Nobody wants to talk about death, but we all know that death is one of the only certainties in life. The more you talk about your wishes and preferences, the decisions that your Health Care Agent may face, and what you would want to happen, the more comfortable and confident your agent and your family will be in a time of need.

Conversation Starters

If you are struggling with how to approach the subject, try one of these conversation starters:

"Did you hear about what happened to [John] when he got sick? What his family went through was just awful. If something happens to me, I don't want you to have to deal with it. I want you to know that I would want...

"I know you don't like talking about death. But it is really important that we do, now, before it is too late. By talking about it now, we can prevent some of the uncertainty and turmoil later.

"I was reading this book by estate planning lawyer Jennifer Lewis Kannegieter, about Health Care Directives and Advance Care Planning. She says it is important for all adults to have a Health Care Directive. I created mine, and now I want to talk to you about my wishes for health care."

What Should You Talk About?

At a very minimum your loved ones should know about your Health Care Directive. But the more guidance you can provide about your wishes, the easier things will be on your family if something were to happen.

Your Health Care Agents need to know they have been selected and should also know about your instructions. But your Health Care Agent will also be bound to follow your wishes, even if they are not contained in the directive, so be sure to talk to your agents about your beliefs and feelings towards life, death, and medical care.

Consider talking to your loved ones about the following:

- Why did you select the Health Care Agents that you did? What strengths do your selected agents have that you feel make them most qualified for the job?

- What do you want your agents to consider when making decisions for you? What would be you top priority?

- How has your experience with others' illnesses and deaths impacted your Health Care Directive? Is there anything you would want to avoid that you have witnessed someone else experience?

- How have your religious and/or spiritual beliefs impacted your advance care planning?

- What are your feelings about different treatment options? What would you like to have tried? What would you like to avoid?

- What are your thoughts about quality of life? How would quality-of-life considerations impact your decisions about medical treatments?

- What words of wisdom or advice would you want to give your agents and/or family during a difficult time in your medical treatment?

- Where would you like to receive care? What medical providers would you choose? What care facility would you want?

- What would you want your family to know at the end of your life?

- What are your thoughts on organ donation? If you wish to be a donor, is there anything you do **not** want to donate?

- After your death, what would you like to happen with your body?

- What are your thoughts about a funeral or memorial service? Where would you want it to take place? Who would you like to speak? What songs or readings would you like?

#7
Make It Accessible

Your Health Care Directive is worthless if it is not there when you need it. Your original Health Care Directive should be kept in a safe place that can be accessed by others. A safe or filing cabinet in your home that your loved ones know about and can access is a good storage location. A safe deposit box at a bank is often inaccessible in an emergency and is not a good place to keep Health Care Directives. Make sure you tell your agents and your family where they can find your Health Care Directive.

You should make copies of your Health Care Directive to give to each of your named Health Care Agents (including alternate agents). You should also give a copy to your doctor, who will make the directive a part of your medical record. Keep a list of everyone who has a copy – this will be handy when it comes time to update your Health Care Directive. If you will be traveling, it is a good idea to bring a copy of your Health Care Directive with you.

Should you maintain any sort of ICE (In Case of Emergency) information on your cell phone or in your wallet, you should also include information about the existence and location of your Health Care Directive.

For added peace of mind, knowing your Health Care Directive will always be there when you need it, consider a service such as DocuBank. With a DocuBank membership, Health Care Directives, medical information, and emergency contact information is stored on secure servers. You are provided an ID card with your unique DocuBank number to keep in your wallet. Emergency personnel can use your DocuBank card to request emergency contact information and a copy of your directive. With a service such as DocuBank your Health Care Directive, emergency contacts, and important medical information will always be accessible.

#8
Review and Update It Regularly

There's no "expiration" date on your Health Care Directive. But it is possible for your directive to become out of date as your life changes. Make it a point to review your Health Care Directive whenever any of the following events happen:

- Five years have passed since the last time you reviewed it.

- There's been a change of address or phone number. It is especially important to keep your Health Care Agents' information current.

- There's been a birth, death, marriage, or divorce in your family that may impact your choice of agents or your wishes.

- There's been a significant change in your health. If you receive a new diagnosis or experience a decline in your condition, it is time to review your Health Care Directive.

When reviewing your Health Care Directive, ask yourself the following questions:

1. Is my address current?

2. Are the right Health Care Agents listed in the appropriate order?

3. Do I have the right contact information for each Health Care Agent?

4. Is there anything I want to change about the powers I am granting my Health Care Agent?

5. Has anything happened to change my instructions? Do I wish to elaborate on anything?

If you determine it is time to update your Health Care Directive, just complete a new form. Make sure it has all of the legally required signatures. Contact everyone who has a copy of your old Health Care Directive and ask them to return the old copy to you so that you can shred it. Provide a copy of the new directive to those who need it and keep a list of everyone you have given a copy.

Appendix A
Additional Resources

If you need more information on advance care planning and Health Care Directives, check out some of the resources below:

Minnesota Health Care Directive Form – We have prepared and provided a free Minnesota Health Care Directive form on our website at: http://www.lewisklaw.com/mnhcd

Honoring Choices Minnesota – Provides resources and videos on advance care planning. www.honoringchoices.com

Minnesota Board on Aging – Provides resources on advance care planning. www.mnaging.org

DocuBank – Provides immediate access to your Health Care Directive. 24/7, 365 days a year. www.docubank.com

National Health Care Decisions Day – Provides information on advance care planning and events held in honor of National Healthcare Decisions Day (April 16th). www.nhdd.org

Appendix B
Free Minnesota Health Care Directive Form and Instructions

Having a Health Care Directive is imperative for *all* adults. A Health Care Directive allows you to appoint an agent to speak for you if you are unable to do so yourself and/or provide instructions for the medical care you wish to receive.

Included here you will find a free Minnesota Health Care Directive form. This form is also available on our website at: www.LewisKLaw.com/mnhcd. This form is designed to be completed entirely on your own. All you need to do is follow the instructions below. If you do need assistance in preparing your Health Care Directive, or if it is time to complete your estate plan, please contact me at (763) 244-2949 or jennifer@lewisklaw.com.

Instructions

Introduction

1. Provide your full legal name (first, middle, and last) under "Minnesota Health Care Directive Of"

2. Complete your personal information, including full name, birth date, address, and phone number.

3. Remember, you must either name a Health Care Agent OR provide Health Care Instructions. You can also do both.

Naming Health Care Agents

4. If you are choosing to appoint Health Care Agents, provide the name, address, and phone number of your primary (first choice) agent.

5. If you wish to appoint alternate agents, who can act if the primary agent is unable to, provide the name, address, and phone number for each alternate agent.

6. If you have named more than one agent to serve as primary agents, first alternate agents, or second alternate agents, decide whether you want the agents to act alone or jointly, and mark the appropriate line.

7. *Note*: If you have named a health care provider or employee of a health care provider who is not related to you, you must provide your reason.

Powers of Your Health Care Agents

8. The next section explains the powers your Health Care Agent(s) will have. The first set of powers are automatically granted.

9. The second set of powers are optional. If you want your Health Care Agent to have any of these powers, check the box next to that power.

10. You can also provide additional powers, or limit the powers granted by filling in the blanks.

Health Care Instructions

11. If you wish to provide Health Care Instructions, you may do so by answering these questions.

12. If you wish to provide an additional page of instructions, initial the line indicating so.

13. *Remember:* You do not have to answer all of the questions, and if you have appointed an agent you do not need to answer any of them. If you have not appointed an agent, you must provide instructions.

Making It Legal

14. Take the completed but unsigned Health Care Directive to either a notary public or two witnesses.

15. The witnesses must be over the age of 18 and must not be appointed as an agent in the document. Only one witness can be a health care provider or employee of a health care provider.

16. In front of the notary public or witnesses, initial the bottom of each and every page. Date and sign. If you are unable to sign for yourself, you can ask another person to sign for you, and print their own name.

17. If you are using a notary public, the notary public should then complete the section for the notary, date, stamp, and sign page 6. If you are using witnesses they should provide their printed name and address, and date and sign.

18. After your Health Care Directive is complete and signed, make copies to distribute to your Health Care Agents, your family, and your doctors. Keep a list of everyone who has a copy. Keep the original in a safe place.

MINNESOTA HEALTH CARE DIRECTIVE OF

Introduction: I have considered my treatment options and personal preferences and have prepared this document if I cannot communicate for myself or make my own health care decisions. I understand this document allows me to name a health care agent to make health care decisions for me if I am unable to decide for myself AND/OR provide health care instructions to guide others in my care decisions.

THIS HEALTH CARE DIRECTIVE SHALL REVOKE ALL PRIOR HEALTH CARE DIRECTIVES, LIVING WILLS, DURABLE POWERS OF ATTORNEY FOR HEALTH CARE, OR OTHER WRITTEN ADVANCE CARE DIRECTIVES.

MY PERSONAL INFORMATION:

Name: _____
Birth Date: _____
Address: _____
_____
Phone: _____

PART 1: NAMING A HEALTH CARE AGENT

My Health Care Agent shall have the power to make health care decisions for me and act on my behalf if I am unable to communicate for myself. My agent must follow my instructions in this document and any other instructions given to my agent. My agent must make decisions that are consistent with my wishes and are in my best interests.

APPOINTMENT OF AGENT(S)

Primary Health Care Agent: If I am unable to communicate for myself, I appoint the following person(s) as my health care agent:

Name: _____
Address: _____
_____
Phone: _____

First Alternate Health Care Agent: If my primary health care agent (named above) is unable or unwilling to serve, I appoint the following person(s) as my health care agent:

Name: _____
Address: _____
_____
Phone: _____

Second Alternate Health Care Agent: If my primary and first alternate health care agents (named above) are unable or unwilling to serve, I appoint the following person(s) as my health care agent:

Name: _____
Address: _____
_____
Phone: _____

If I have named more than one agent, it is my desire that the agents:

____ Act Alone: Only one agent is needed to act
____ Act Jointly: ALL agents must act together and agree on treatment

If I have named a health care provider or employee of a health care provider who is not related to me as a health care agent, I have done so for the following reason: _____

POWERS OF MY HEALTH CARE AGENT:

If I am unable to speak for myself, my Health Care Agent has the power to:

- Make any health care decision for me, when, in the judgment of my attending physician, I lack decision-making capacity. This includes the power to give, refuse, or withdraw consent to any care, treatment, service, or procedure. My agent has the power to stop or not start care that is keeping me alive or might keep me alive. This shall include all types of mental health treatment.
- Choose my health care providers and care facilities.
- Choose where I live when I need health care and determine what personal security measures are needed for my safety.
- Review my medical records and have the same rights that I would have to allow other people access to my medical records. My Health Care Agent shall be treated as my personal representative for purposes of the Health Insurance Portability and Accountability Act of 1996 (HIPAA). I waive all medical privilege in favor of any agent and personal representative I appoint under this document.

Additional Powers of My Health Care Agent:
(If I want my Health Care Agent to have any of the following powers, I will check the box in front of each statement below.)

I also authorize my Health Care Agent to:

- Make health care decisions for me even if I am able to decide or speak for myself, if I so choose.

- Arrange for and make decisions about the care of my body after death and carry out my wishes regarding a burial, cremation, funeral, or memorial service.

- In the event I am pregnant, determine whether to continue my pregnancy to delivery based upon my agent's understanding of my values and preferences.

- In the event of a court proceeding for a guardian to have authority concerning life-sustaining procedures or other health care for me, I nominate, pursuant to Minnesota Statutes, my Health Care Agent(s) named in this document to be appointed by the court as my guardian.

- If I have named a spouse or domestic partner, to continue as my Health Care Agent even if a dissolution, annulment, or termination of our marriage or domestic partnership is in process or has been completed.

- Additional powers or restrictions for my Health Care Agent: _____

_____

PART 2: HEALTH CARE INSTRUCTIONS

My instructions and preferences for my health care are as follows. I ask my agent and doctors to honor them in case I am unable to communicate them myself.

General Preferences: I have the following general preferences for my health care:

_____
_____
_____

Specific Instructions: I have the following instructions for my health care:

_____
_____
_____

Location for Care: I have the following preferences for where I receive care:

_____
_____

Is Life Worth Living? I have the following beliefs about when life would no longer be worth living and what is most important to me:

_____
_____
_____

Additional Thoughts: I have the following thoughts and feelings about health care, end-of-life care, and death:

_____
_____
_____

Terminal Condition Instructions: I have the following instructions if I am in a terminal condition:

- o I do want all appropriate treatments and procedures as reasonably recommended by my doctor until my doctor and agent decide such treatments are harmful or no longer helpful.

- I do NOT want treatments and procedures that will not substantially improve my condition or help me recover, but will only postpone the moment of my death.

- If it is reasonably certain I will not recover my ability to know who I am, I wish to be allowed to die naturally and not be kept alive by artificial means or heroic measures.

- Other instructions for terminal condition: _____
  _____
  _____

Organ Donation: I have the following wishes regarding organ donation after death.

- I DO NOT wish to donate my organs, tissue, eyes, and/or other body parts

- I DO wish to donate my organs, tissue, eyes, and/or other body parts when I die.

    - I wish to donate anything and everything that could be used
    - I wish to donate everything EXCEPT
      _____
      _____

    - I ONLY wish to donate:
      _____
      _____

- I wish the donation to be made to: _____
  _____

- I do not want my donated organs to be used for: ____
  _____

My Body After Death: After my death, I want:

- To be cremated
- To be buried
- To donate my body to:
- For my agent to decide
- Other instructions for my body after death:

Additional Instructions Attached. If I have attached additional instructions concerning my health care values and preferences, I have initialed here: _____

PART 3: LEGALLY REQUIRED SIGNATURES

Under Minnesota law, to be a valid legal document this Health Care Directive must be signed and dated in the presence of two witness OR a notary public.

I have made this document willingly. I am thinking clearly and I agree with everything that is written in this document. This document accurately reflects my wishes and preferences for future medical care.

Date: _____   _____
                                              Signature

If I cannot sign my name, I ask the following person to sign for me:

_____
Printed name of person asked to sign:

_____
Signature of person asked to sign:

Notary Public

STATE OF MINNESOTA   )
) ss.
COUNTY OF _____   )

Subscribed, sworn to, and acknowledged before me by _____ on this ____ day of _____ 20___. I am not named as a health care agent or alternate health care agent in this document.

Notary Stamp or Seal   _____
                                              Notary Public

OR

Two Witnesses

I personally witnessed the signing of this document. I am not an agent or alternate agent appointed in this agreement.

First Witness:

_____   _____
Date   Signature

Printed Name: _____

Address: _____

If I am a health care provider or an employee of a health care provider providing care to the person named above, I must initial here: _____

I personally witnessed the signing of this document. I am not an agent or alternate agent appointed in this agreement.

Second Witness:

_____   _____
Date   Signature

Printed Name: _____

Address: _____

If I am a health care provider or an employee of a health care provider providing care to the person named above, I must initial here: _____

About The Author

Jennifer R. Lewis Kannegieter, is a mother, an estate planning and family law attorney, founding lawyer at Lewis Kannegieter Law, Ltd., and *Your Minnesota Family Lawyer*.

She understands that estate planning is about more than wills and trusts. She takes a *Total Estate Planning* approach considering all aspects of a clients' financial, emotional, and physical estate planning needs. She helps her clients prepare for whatever life may bring their way.

Jennifer R. Lewis Kannegieter

She takes a three-pronged approach to her practice based on the importance of family, education, and common sense. She maintains an extensive directory of resources on her firm's website and is active in community education efforts. Jennifer has authored many articles on estate planning, family law, and working with lawyers and she frequently speaks on these topics. Jennifer resides in Monticello, Minnesota with her family where she is an active member of the community. For more information visit her website at www.LewisKLaw.com.

www.ingramcontent.com/pod-product-compliance
Lightning Source LLC
Chambersburg PA
CBHW061519180526
45171CB00001B/243